Ambiguous
Parables

Ambiguous Parables

Poems and Prose
of Loss and Renewal

Ted Bowman

NODIN PRESS

9 8 7 6 5 4 3

ISBN: 978-1-947237-36-0
Library of Congress Control Number: 2021947554

Published by
Nodin Press
5114 Cedar Lake Road,
Minneapolis, MN 55416
www.nodinpress.com

Printed in USA

To my wife,
Marge Grahn-Bowman
December 1940 – July 2020

Table of Contents

Introduction and Acknowledgements

THE COLLECTED PROSE and poetic pages herein are the voice of a man seeking greater comfort with ambiguity. What seems to be is not always what is. A life-long quest has been to find words—the words of others through conversations, poetry, song lyrics, fiction, non-fiction, scriptures—and/or my own words, to acknowledge and address ambiguous experiences. To find, years ago, these lines in James Baldwin's *Another Country,* resonated and affirmed my quest. "One is never what one seems—never—and yet, what one seems to be is probably, in some sense, almost exactly what one is."

These pages affirm mystery, celebrate ambiguity, and affirm ever-changing lives.

While many of the pieces are personal, I remind you, the reader, through the words of Frederick Buechner: "My story is important not because it is mine, God knows, but because if I tell it anything like right, the chances are you will recognize that in many ways it is also yours." (from *Telling Secrets: A Memoir*)

I acknowledge that I am by disposition, training, and a lifetime of work an educator-poet. You will find that many of the poems and prose pieces herein include an introduction, story and commentary or response. Some poet friends have attempted to alter my voice. Their support and inputs have strengthened, shortened, and informed my writing, for which I am grateful. Still, one's voice is one's voice. I especially salute and thank Norita Dittberner-Jax, Michael Dennis Browne, Dara Syrkin, and the late Carol Bly for their supportive inputs.

Apart from two sections in this volume, the flow for the poems and prose is neither chronological nor themed. Rather, the order was chosen to reveal various external and internal prompts to find words.

This volume was enriched by my first reader, Marge my wife, who for 41 years supported me and my writing. Her presence kept me grounded and open to each day and the next. I miss her greatly since her sudden death in 2020. A tribute poem to her starts the volume.

Further salutes go to my extended family and friends who accepted my writing with grace as Ted's thing; he writes.

The work of colleagues and friends who use literary resources for healing (poetry therapists and bibliotherapists) in the United States, England, and Scotland also deserve saluting. I had the honor of serving on the board of the National Association for Poetry Therapy and speaking and leading workshops for Lapidus UK and Lapidus Scotland.

And a further appreciation to Norton Stillman, long-time friend of Minnesota poets, for his previous publishing of two co-edited volumes and our occasional conversations about our lives and our work.

The cover art is the creation of Newcastle, England, artist Jacqueline Quinn, friend and colleague. The piece in entitled Illuminate. Her web sites are: *www.jacquelinequinnart.com* and *www.facebook.com/artjacquelinequinn*

Ambiguous Parables

I Will Color This Time

I will color this time
With more than a black arm band,
A past marker of death

I will reach for brilliant, bold, bright colors
and
Beiges, blues and blush

I yearn for an array of color
Similar to the rainbow of flowers
Sent so soon after her death
Reminding me of the colorful life we shared
...and I can still have

What One Seems

I
Sometime since then and there
The dreams,
Planted as perennials,
Turned out to be annuals instead.

II
Sometime between there and then and here and now
The rules changed
Male expectations evolved
The man I am
Faced a crossroads

III
Sometimes in the midst of here and now
My there and then shows up.
Generations appear in one body.
I listen attentively,
Past and present overlap and collide

IV
The man I am
Can, from this distance, see
Ways the boy I was got here.
The boy, looking ahead,
Would have thought this man strange.

The Man with a Hat

I have been called many things,
But this name was strange
The woman who called it out
Knew without hesitation that her
Barking dog was saying
Oh, it's the man with a hat

She must be a dog-whisperer
A canine language interpreter
Her statement was confident
There was no speculation
She loudly told her neighbor what was said

For this label, I did not feel chagrined
You know, *men who wear hats*
Rather, my steps were lighter
Even quicker
Not to escape the dog or her
I considered of all the names
Her dog could have said,
I welcomed
That naming that day at that spot

Unexpected Writer

"You think you are the only writer, don't you?" was the greeting from my dad. Said with a smile and the tone of expectancy, I curiously awaited what was to come. And out it tumbled: a pile of yellow pages with turned-up corners, full of hand-written words, thrust in my direction by the proud writer. "Look at this," he said.

Little did I know that the written version of this man's life and legacy was now in my hands. Unbeknownst to me, my brothers, and most astoundingly, our mother, Dad had found seclusion and creativity in a writer's den he created in the storage shed behind our parents' home. Steadily over a year and more, he had written his life story on these now marked and stained pages.

"Would you type it for me?" he asked, inviting me to provide him with a service that would give more to the typist than either of us expected. "Yes, of course," I replied. Later, after returning home, I began to read and type this gift. Part memoir, part essay and sermon, the pages contained a life story of poverty, hope, the American dream, faith and family. It was honest, poignant, and full of the man I called Dad.

I've received many things from my father over the years: ties and mugs, shirts, and books, but no gift came close to matching the power of his life story. There are too many accounts of parents who keep the doors closed to shaping influences of their early years. Decisions made that changed the course of lives can be buried along with a person. In his memoir, *Growing Up*, Russell Baker described this tendency: *Children rarely want to know who their parents were before they were parents, and when age finally stirs their curiosity there is no parent left to tell them. If a parent does lift the curtain a bit, it is often only to stun the young with some exemplary tale of how much harder life was in the old days.* Fortunately, my father didn't wait until it was too late.

Dad's tale was exemplary, and it did contain stories of hard living. The intent was not to regale the reader. Even more important than the details were his actions of doing the writing. Some narratives deserve more than memory. And words on paper can be read again. And again. Even long after his death, I can take a part of him off the shelf and read.

What makes it all the more special was the surprise. This man was no writer. He was a talker. I have very few letters or notes from him because he wrote so few. For him to write anything, especially his memoir, took special effort and love. Some stories are hard to write because of their content. Some others are hard to write because the author has little experience putting words on paper. Somehow Dad put pencil to yellow paper, the collection of which he waved in my face that day, months after he started writing.

No, I'm not the only writer in the family.

Quote from *Growing Up* (1982) by Russell Baker. New York: Congdon & Weed, Inc.

An Unscheduled Day

What does one do with an unscheduled day?
To treat it as a gift implies few chores
No to the prospect of a project
Depth of thought is for other days
A to-do list is an everyday roster
Not for an unscheduled gift day

For hours I meander
Sipping tea looking at the snow fall
Am I to be a voyeur of a snowstorm?
The gift of the day remains unwrapped

I meander more

A jazz trio plays in the background
Improvisation noted as they pass
Tunes from one to the other
Handing notes to another to build on
Impressed I sit awaiting my turn
Hoping I will know what to do when
My turn comes to improvise on
"An Unscheduled Day"

Acorns, Bcorns and Ccorns

The botanical consultant
Directed attention to the object of his study
A patch of grass covered by acorns
Shadowed by the aging parent oak
He picked acorns for closer study
They're not all the same, Grandpa
Look this one is green; that one brown
This one has no cap
Where is the cap?
Here's a double, two together,
How do they do that?

Buckets were found
We began gathering and sorting
Look-alikes assigned their own homes
Grandpa, these are not all acorns
They are not all alike
Grandpa, some are bcorns
Others ccorns
How do we decide which are which?

I had, without much thought,
Signed up for this research project
When my daughter was pregnant
Had there been fine print, I would have read
"When one becomes a grandpa a paradigm shifts
Be prepared for questions."
Little did I know that being a grandpa
Means seeing acorns differently
This upper-level course
Was taught by a botanist with no shingle or degree but
         with eyes, thoughts and questions
I wish more of my earlier teachers had said, *Grandpa, look*

Safe Places

As children
Our games included safe places:
Bases where we were safe and free
Lines that the monster intruder could not cross
Areas off limits, out of the games
Parents around whose legs we wrapped ourselves yelling,
"You can't get me, I'm safe here!"

Now older
I'm still looking for safe places.
But, the fears inside
Seem to know the safe places I seek.
They wait there patiently for my arrival,
Courage and faith, my only legs left to stand on.

Imagined Places

As children
Our games included imagined places
Where, for as long as the game lasted,
We were smart, strong, and in charge.
In those brief moments
Possibilities overcame barriers
The world was ours.

Now older
I still play the same game
Hoping that before my time expires
I can be smarter, stronger and in charge
Just long enough for
Imagination to open its doors
Inviting me through.

Home Places

As children
We played house.
Sometimes I was the father,
Often a child,
Now and then a teacher or cop.
Our house had many doors

Now older
I know that home is more than place.
Still…place,
A loving place,
Place that you can count on
Makes a house a home
I hope my children play house
In their homes.

Marked Places

As children
We colored inside the lines
Black was black and white was white
Invisible markers segregated neighborhoods
But eyes saw, all knew
The currency of that time
Robbed neighbors of neighbors

Later, I met someone from there
She could have been my childhood playmate
We had much in common
Love of reading, tennis, families
We agreed that separated, distinct childhoods
Robbed us of each other, marking us for life

Now older
Two grandparents
Eagerly show photos of grandchildren
Who behave in once unimaginable ways
Coloring outside the lines of our childhood
We stare at each other
Invisible markers still there
The intersection of privilege and history

Life Happens

Life happens as you make other plans
Came to mind as the train sped from London to Edinburgh
Six decades earlier on a North Carolina dirt road
A boy, riding his bike,
Abruptly slowed, then stopped
His pant leg caught in the bicycle chain
The boy, far, far from home
Knew better than to rip the trousers free
His best school britches
So, he walked one-legged toward home
A journey that seemed as far to him
As London to Edinburgh

That boy never envisioned riding a train
Anywhere
His world was more narrow
His people spoke what he thought was English
And the only queen he knew was his mother
Travel? Maybe over the hill into the next county
Never another state or country…except
In his imagination,
With Jack London, he knew that London
Adventure writer, *The Call of the Wild*
Together they traveled far into the Yukon

Now on a train from London to Edinburgh
He pulled up his britches
Caught in the chain of memories and horizons

The Message

(With appreciation to the French poet
Jacques Pre'vert's (1900-1977) poem
The Message (*Le Message*)

The place someone dreamed
The door someone opened
The chair someone sat in
The cat someone stroked
The fruit someone bit on
The text someone read
The views some god created
The roads someone traveled
The tea someone sipped
The garden someone nurtured
The touch someone offered
The deep sleep someone slept
The friendship someone encouraged
The place someone made welcoming
The place someone called safe
Home

A borrowed and adapted poem
written for The Center for Victims of Torture

Old Hands

The familiar spiritual space
Was altered as I looked as never before
At my hands, my obviously old hands.

It was Maundy Thursday, a sacred day for Christians
The last supper for Jesus and his disciples
Tradition includes food and drink
And the washing of feet by Jesus
An intimate act of compassion and service

For the Thursday I have in mind
Hands not feet would be washed
Two persons, taking turns,
Washing the other's hands

When I wash my hands
I seldom look as I did that day
My hands were old, a reminder of
My father now dead almost fourteen years

These hands were mine
Embarrassed until my partner
Simply washed my hands
It was intimate; it was healing
Altering my sense of self

Poems as Mom Declined and Died

My mom died in 2009. During the last eight years of her life, she moved further and further into the fog of dementia. We lost our mother before we lost our mother. The poems in this section were written during that time and after she died.

Early in her life, she developed a fondness for cardinals, a passion she sustained lifelong. I post one here to honor Bertie Bowman.

Soften the Blow

For Bertie

The Alzheimer's came first
Later came the stroke
Robbing her diamonds and pearls
She lost the past
And her left side
The stories she loved
And her mobility
Still she smiled
I love you
Thank you, dear
You're a handsome fellow
So good
Your hands feel so warm
She loved us all
Grandchildren, nurses, friends

A smile can soften the blow
Especially a genuine love of people
And of life

No doubt there was grief, loneliness, and abject fear
But those she kept tucked away
Not for public display
Allowing her smile to fill the room

It makes her dying harder
And easier
Our tears blend with smiles
Grief and unexpected joy overflow

When One Says Little

When one says little
Twinkles, grimaces, and nods magnify
The little shown or said
Grows in memory and meaning.
Whatever you can get is acceptable
Even when more is desired.

Dementia had taken
Mom's vocabulary
Her stories and comments have shrunk
To a word or phrase here
A frown or giggle there
Forcing me to listen and watch
For any wrinkle or word.

We hang onto:
So good,
Come closer
That hurts
Don't go
Interpreting each as if we could read
The ever-changing, limited mind of Mom

He's looking at me,
Was heard one day as she and a calendar dog
Engaged in a stand-off of staring.
She held her ground and gaze;
Which blinked first is unknown

I came to believe that she was still the teacher
Reminding her sons, like the dog, to see her.
She didn't say *Look at me*
She had rarely been that direct
No, when we appeared
She lifted her slumped head

Looked…paused… said
My, my, you are a handsome fellow!
Her compliment,
The best phrase said that day.
It mirrored what I believe to have been a deep yearning
To also be seen
By dog or person
Especially for those who can only say
…or know a little

Pilgrimage Home

I called my mom this evening.
Nothing new, this Sunday ritual.
Long ago, calls became our weekend routine.
Like before, we exchanged greetings,
News, love, what we were doing.
Then, her consistent exclamation:
'Your call has made my day!'
Sadness followed.
Not because our call was brief,
Nor due to the distance between us.
No, my mom won't remember this call.
Usually this does not distress me.
For years now, we have shared her Alzheimer's.

Tonight, however, I wanted her to remember Iona.
Iona, place of memory, island of history,
Land of deep roots.
I wanted mom to know I was here.
For centuries, pilgrims have come and gone
From this hard and lovely place.
Her pilgrimage is almost over;
She has come to the edge of being gone,
Of coming home.
Still her delight when I told her tonight
Will be similar to the joy
When I tell her again next Wednesday

Sometimes pilgrims need neither a history
Nor a destination.
Sometimes moments of delight suffice.
I came to Iona to learn something.
I did, now I remember,
Call home;
That's where all pilgrimages begin.

The Day the Music Died

Say aloud the title of this poem,
Especially to persons of a certain age,
You will likely hear names:
Buddy Holly, Richie Valens, and the "Big Bopper",
Their death in a plane crash
Remembered and memorialized by another name,
Don McLean.

Say aloud the title of this poem
To three brothers, three sons
You will likely hear the name, Bertie,
Our mom
We, too, remember the day the music died

My brother brought music on his iPod
Her favorite hymns, gospel music, old favorites
Her dementia and old age,
Caused each of us to wonder
If she still fully heard when we spoke
She was often unresponsive, silent
Ambiguity our experience, perhaps hers,
Until the sounds of music filled her ears

She smiled
She moved her head to and fro
Bertie's face changed
Three brothers sighed
The music ended
My brother removed her headphones
He spoke for each of us
"Mom, we brought some of your favorite music
We love you"

Then, we heard her final spoken words to us,
"I love you, too"
It was the day the music died.

Reason Enough

What does one say to a grandson in a coma
Or a mom living in a dementia fog
Questions go unanswered
Efforts unacknowledged

You stand by the bedside
Sit in the adjacent chair
You saddle up close
Touch an arm, say some words

You yearn for responses
Some movement of lip
Eyebrow lifting, head tilting
It's a mystery what can be heard
What it's like in there?
Ambiguity abounds

One day, Mom came out of the fog
Lifted her face toward mine
Smiled…
"I knew you would be here"

One of those in a lifetime
Is reason enough
To stand, sit, cajole
Gift given, gift received

My mom is dying

I who have sat at bedsides of the dying

I who teach about grief and end of life

I who am supposed to know what I talk about

I whose professional strengths are now fragile

My mom is dying

Through the depression to the millennial

Through tough times to this threshold

Through fixed roles to quiet leadership

Through it all she smiled, lifting spirits

My mom is dying

We have said our words

We have done our deeds

We have emulated her caring in our care of her

We have been faithful sons

My mom is dying

She has been released

She has received our love

She believes in what waits for her

Her journey is ending and beginning

My mom is dying

The Captain

My boss is seven years old. This is not a startling arrangement. Some years ago the new minister at my church was younger than I. It was then that I released age as an essential quality for leadership. I had thought the older you were, the wiser. The distance from younger ministers and managers to seven-year-old bosses is not wide.

My seven-year-old grandson is the captain. I'm the matey. He first announced this arrangement when he was four. So, I now have three years of seniority over any new mates that might be designated or found. Mine is a position of privilege because when he became the captain there were no other mateys. I remain the only one. My wife has a unique role, but she is not a matey. She is Toots, an appreciative term for one who shows due respect to the captain and who does not interfere with the captain and his matey.

I've had many bosses over the years, but none like the captain. He is clearer than most of my supervisors were about plans and who is in charge. There is no boundary ambiguity; he is the captain. While we work together on some projects—abstract drawing for example—the ultimate choice of colors or theme, if there is one, is his to make. I know my place. He knows his.

While there is no pay, there are substantial benefits. My captain is a teacher. His values, preferences and the treatment of subordinates are congruent and consistent. He is more direct than most of my bosses have been. He believes that I can learn from my mistakes and successes, each of which he notes as we work together.

He also affirms me with handshakes, hugs, and incredibly rich smiles or grins. I leave renewed and full of joy each time I work with the captain. Most important, there is a loyalty covenant between the captain and his worker that invites reciprocity.

Would-be corporate managers and aspiring organization consultants could forego MBA programs, saving time and money, by spending time with seven-year-olds. Valuable work and life lessons can be learned about balancing work and play, power, clarity of direction, of respect for those in leadership roles, and about humility. I think I'm getting what they call life-long learning. Too bad it took a long life for this boss to arrive and offer the position.

My London Neighborhood

How does one say good-bye to a place he has loved?
I looked up at the flats above the shops
The shops I know by name, use, and satisfaction
The one where I buy my newspapers and chocolates
The laundry that has helped me be presentable
The pubs and the restaurants, banks and posts
The meandering streets toward Russell Square Park
And so much I don't know, that I will never know
Who lives in those flats?

I know change; the Italian restaurant is now French
A small Tesco's arrived since I began coming here
The place I used to exchange money and get stamps
Now a well-known brand of coffee shop

Most familiar is the Harlingford Hotel
My home away from home
For more than two decades
I have known their closet-sized rooms
If I turn around in the shower
Water will splash over the whole bathroom
I also know the woman
That has poured my coffee and toasted my bread
For as long as I have stayed there
She smiled at me then; she smiles at me now

I crave stability when traveling,
Here I am, maybe the last time
I walk slowly, look up, across and inside
I who never thought of being in London
Have been here more than most places
How does one take a neighborhood with him?
How does one say goodbye to a place one loves?

Release

To my right are 241 books of poetry
Some dog-eared; others hardly opened
To my left are writing projects to be done
Journals yet unread alongside files and clutter
Directly in front is a screen and keyboard
Ready for fingers to do their thing

Others have sat in this chair
Waiting for the writing light to turn green
I turn to my right
And hear Billy Collins tell me
To wash my study before composing a syllable
The more you clean, the more brilliant the writing
I recall Leslie Monsour's practice of
Enjoying poems other people write
Find Alice Munro rifling around in the past
Because it's what people do
Linda Pastan asserts that finding a new poet
Is like finding a new wildflower out in the woods.
William Stafford starting writing before daylight
It's now mid-afternoon

A voice is heard, W. S. Merwin, I believe
Inside this pencil
crouch words that have never been written
never been spoken
never been taught

they're hiding

I speak to my pencil
Come out, come out wherever you are
I am finally ready to release you

Lines from W.S. Merwin's "The Unwritten"

Naïve Betrayal

She saw him at a place he frequented
Naiveté, majority privilege
Led her to misunderstand and overlook
What could happen when he was outed
By her account to his colleagues

Their previously strong relationship
Now in shambles
Mistrust the dominant narrative
"I cannot work with her!"
And his righteous announcement
"I will not"

She desperately tried to pull words said
From the heart of her poisoned colleague

Trust is a rock
Sitting on quicksand
Their relationship was sinking
The sand in her mouth
Rock ready to throw in his hand

I was privy to a parable
A parable about the power of words
A tale about boundaries
Trust in relationships is a rocky road
Step care-fully, speak caringly
Whose story was this to tell?

Thorough

I had met her kind before
Often on trains like this
One row in front, to my left,
Across the aisle she sat
Thoroughly reading the paper
I observed her consuming
Article by article, page by page
The news of that day
She, a connoisseur
Page turning was paced, not hurried

I wondered about her opinions
What perspectives
Were evoked by such thoroughness
She brought years of life to
Whatever she might write or say
In her daily editorial column
To share her company in this
The quiet car, lifted my hopes
Accounts of troubles across the globe
Could be addressed if more, like her,
Would choose to be thoroughly informed

After leaving railcar D
I stopped and bought a paper

Teeter-Totters and Caring

When one is sick,
Especially chronically ill
The tendency is for attention and care
To be offered in one direction

Standing over there
Just out of the picture
Stands another.
Sometimes called caregiver
Friend
Often spouse.

Whether offered with grace
Or resentment
This one too deserves care
Sickness in families is a teeter-totter
Requiring balance and movement
Between two and more
Between highs and lows

My friend knows how to teeter-totter
He is, in fact, one of the best
Sometimes digging in his feet
Grounding his wife and all riders
Sometimes rising and falling with us
To places and possibilities never expected

Male Tears

Tears well up and seek surface drainage.
Blocked by poor priming,
Inexperience,
Rocky soil,
They reluctantly return to their storage place
To await a plumber.

A Man's Tears

Tears well up from pools of pain,
Desiring to do what they are supposed to do,
Seek surface drainage.
The troubled waters exert pressure upward,
But clogged pipes,
Corroded by disuse,
Block their flow toward release.

A man's plumber resides within.
His handyman kit ready,
If and when the manhole cover is lifted.

Aunt Frances

I've been wondering about Aunt Frances,
Curious about her parts
And what the medical students learned from her
When she died at age 91
Her children gave her body to science
As they had been directed

I can't imagine that she just lay on the table,
The medical students gathered around,
For the teaching day about older bodies
I'm certain she sat up and told those students
A thing or two
About persons, not diseases
To avoid patronizing condescension
The importance of story gathering
Meet patients where they are
Spend a bit of time with each

She would have said it straight
With a gleam in her eyes
And with a smile that would have softened her students.
Few would have met someone like her, alive or dead,
Because they did, their practices will never be the same

Changing Places

I saw it first through her eyes
That's how it often happens
The storyteller's story includes places

It was a place of grief and pain
It was a place that reminded her of all she had lost
It was a place she got to know too well

It was also a place of hope
It was a place where she found her voice
      Writing in ways she had dreamed about
It became a community place
      She met people she would never have known
      And after knowing them
Would have regretted not meeting

She took me to this place
First through stories and poems and more stories
Then she took my hand and brought me to see
      To meet
      To experience
The wonder when a place unknown, even off-putting
Becomes familiar
And when something familiar becomes another home

(Lombardi Cancer Center in Washington D.C. was the place. It included a writing center program.)

Caregiving

(adapted phrases and words heard from caregivers)

Chronic caring
Caring chronologically

Acceptance
Doesn't mean
Approval

Vows imply
More verbs
Than nouns

It's not what I pictured
Neither was this last winter

Look both ways
Care-receiver
Care-giver
It's a crossroads

I took
Whatever
You could give
It was enough

Grief
Is not the enemy
It's a messenger

I present
My presence
It's the only
Present left

Remembering
Re–membering
Memories
Memories lost
A couple stood together
Strange pair then
Strangers now

Caregiver burden
Depends

When Traveling Across Borders

Once in an elegant, English restaurant
Four men in expansive conversation
Lifted glasses, shared a lovely meal
All supported by an ever-present waiter
Never hovering, always attentive
Until all finished their meals
The waiter nowhere to be found
Until, my host and friend, with proper delicacy
Gently suggested that I place knife and fork
In a particular arrangement on my plate

As soon as I did
The plates were cleared, tea and coffee poured
The sweets were offered
I, a sophisticated traveler, did not know
The subtle, proper gesture to announce
One has completed his English meal

When traveling across borders
Be aware of the local customs
Be prepared to be embarrassed
Humility is welcomed in most countries

Distinctions

(We interrupt this regularly scheduled program for breaking news...)

My pupils widened,
Straining to see what I did not want to see
While their eyes burning or raw with dust
Struggled to see some way out

My ears became dog-like,
Hearing sounds not heard before
While the roar of engines, crumbling buildings
And screaming drummed in their heads

My feelings heightened AND numbed
Just as they experienced emotions no one should ever face

My lungs gasped; easy breathing interrupted
Their lungs filled with fire, smoke, and dust

My stomach turned
Too many had eaten their last meal

My tear ducts opened
About the time their air ducts collapsed

My thoughts wandered hither and yon
Their realizations became crystal clear

My body froze in place
Their bodies were cremated

My heart broke
Theirs stopped beating

My life was turned upside down
A building imploded on theirs

I observed
They experienced

I wanted to do something/anything
Their choices were limited

I had distance
They were too, too close for comfort

These distinctions are crucial
Still we were joined and always will be
Death of this kind is contagious
I will always live with it

(Begun 9/11/01)

Fatherhood

Is it something one assumes, becomes, or earns?
Does it happen at conception, birth, acknowledgment,
        or the moment of choice?

Who confers it: the child, society, the other parent, oneself?

Once begun, does it continue? Is it temporary? Does it
        come and go?
Can one be more of, yes, even less of a father?

How will I know when I become one?
Tell me how it feels. How does one prepare?

Questions, gushing from deep inside as
Boys becoming men add to their role collection
A role so awesome the strongest can cringe in fright
And for which the weakest muster and discover courage
        never felt before

Fatherhood: whether birth, step, gay, adoptive, grand or foster
Can when assumed, chosen or acknowledged,
Not to mention if earned or conferred,
Become the most humbling, curious, unpredictable,
        exciting, warm, demanding giving, liberating
Experience known to man

The Walk

The walk was with her through forest and fields
Autumn filled nostrils
Horses to the left, sheep to the right
We stepped on stones across streams
Over fence gates and fallen trees, surrounded by bleats,
        neighs and caws, crunching and conversation,
All competing for attention

It was exactly
What he and I would have loved to do. It had become our
        ritual
An almost annual rite to walk and talk, the noble Englishman
And his American companion
Rarely a dog, only we two

For over two years now
He has walked uphill into Parkinson's stepping on uneven
        ground
Grief on the one side, hope on the other
Tests and procedures leading to ambiguity just over the next
        hill
None of it as attractive as sunsets in autumn

I'm glad she and I walked
It was our first
Not to be our last
Somehow it seemed a salute
To him and our score-long ritual

I'm glad the three of us did it

A Year of Poems – After Chris Died

My grandson, Chris, died in April 2017. Even as he was dying, I decided that I would write for at least one year following his death. In this section are selected pieces from that year. The cover art is also placed here. Artist Jacqueline Quinn titled her work *Illuminate*.
That was my quest during the year of writing.

The Call

The one that sucks all the air
Pulling oxygen out
Oxygen, I discover
My grandson needs to stay alive

I can hardly hear my son's voice
He, too, tries to breathe
The call in the night that stole
His serenity, our hope
That neither he nor I
Would make or receive such a call

Details pile up
But only one essential detail
My grandson may not live the night
Thoughts churned
My zest for life collapsing

Children are not supposed to die first
Grandchildren even less so
The call
Continues to ring
Long after we have hung up

Written the week of April 24, 2017

Two Weeks Ago

Actually, two weeks and eighteen hours ago
Looking in from the outside
You might not notice differences of routine
I work, do laundry, pay bills, and read the paper
The paper not as fully or closely as usual
You might not know that; I do

I am aware day and night
My life has changed; death does that
Especially a grandson's death
My intentions of the last three weeks
Altered, awaiting action
That has its weight and burden
Focus also, that has been my challenge
Strange, at times I'm keenly focused
Productive, in a zone, doing well
At others I drift, wander, wonder
And wail

I know that about loss and grief
But knowledge didn't stop Chris from using
And knowledge alone cannot feed my soul
So, I turn to poetry, to nature
Allow myself to fully receive the condolences
From close friends and surprising strangers
Today I talked with college graduates about loss
Urged them, like Rumi, to welcome loss
The human guest house can be hospitable
Even for the uninvited and unwanted

This epistle is an attempt to welcome my guests
And to grieve again what occurred
Two weeks and eighteen hours ago

    Written on the second week anniversary of a grandson's death

Severe Clear

The prompt for the bi-monthly writing group was
Where were you when…a world changing event occurred?
Some came prepared with the first step on the moon
Kennedy's assassination in Dallas
I thought of the sit-in at Woolworth's in Greensboro
Most remembered September Eleventh

One person brought the September 24, 2001 *New Yorker*
With one line from the beginning of an article
"The day began with what pilots' call
Severe clear – seemingly infinite visibility"
We were urged to write with whatever the sentence
        prompted

Immediately, the lyrics of a song were in my mouth
"I can see clearly now", by Johnny Nash.
It kept playing in my head, stuck on the first line
No further lines emerged, only that one
I sang it discreetly while others wrote

I saw clearly Chris on life support
The same young man I will never see again
I yearn for severe clear
That will unravel the mystery of his too-early death
Instead, I am left with a wobbling faith
About assumptions, expectations and dreams
About choices, friends and drugs
About family and friends who looked but did not see
I yearn for the lines I cannot remember

In reality, I cannot see clearly now
My vantage is blurred, blocked and bereft
My vantage is severe, not clear

– May 2017

Bulk, Bulk Up

My grandson had often spoken about bulk
It was a common term when he gave me his update:
Weight gained, weights lifted, and rotations done
Last week I bulked grief
The size and weight surpassed all previous losses
My body ached for days; it still does
I didn't think I had it in me
It was as if I was in a gym
Moving from one regimen to another

There are many metaphors for grief
A hole, empty bed, and roller coaster
All attempts to find words for losses
Until last week, I had not thought of bulk
My athletic grandson gave me a new metaphor
I would not call it a gift
But when a grandson dies, the grief has bulk
That fills one's body, life, one's world
I had few muscles for this challenge

When I bulk
I would prefer to do so voluntarily
Chips, chocolate and chilled beer
Come to mind; I know them well
I would even lift some weights
Work out on rowing machines
For my health or by doctor's orders
But don't ask me to bulk up on grief

– May 2017

Letting Go

At the funeral I heard bits of stories
Tantalizing ties to my grandson then and now
I wanted to step from the reception line
Take this person and that to a private space
Desperate to better know my grandson
His demons, desires, and direction

I must let him go
I must not allow his addictive life
Override the grand boy / man he was
There is a whole life to review
I yearn to fully see him

A unknown mentor taught me a hard lesson:
"I don't know why
I'll never know why
I don't have to know why
I don't like it
What I have to do
Is to make a choice about my own living"

– June 2017

Three Months Later

Today is one of those dates that had no significance
Until a fateful day three months ago
And a modest date now stands out

Coincidentally two days ago was also significant
Thirty-eight years ago, we got married
Now dates, two days apart loom large
In hearts, minds and memories

When does the counting begin and end
For now, noting the months serves
As a reminder of his crash from life

Causes me to pause, consider
Relationships, values, and choices
Consider his twenty-three years
And my part of each one

This is not a poem about guilt
I'm wrestling, as he did
As the poet did
With her haunting question

Tell me, what is it you plan to do
with your one wild and precious life?

– July 2017

The last two lines are from a Mary Oliver poem, 'The Summer
Day"

Flooded

My son flew today to Texas
To do whatever would be required
Rescue, behind the scene support,
Toting bags of rice, sand and friendship
Waiting for his assignment
Facing the Texas floods
No matter, David will be ever-ready

I'm thrilled my son can help others
When helping one's own
Was not received, perhaps not possible
He tried, oh, he tried
In his own manly way
He and his son floating past each other
In the bayous of father and son
His son was out of reach

I hope for clarity in Texas
Not found in the Tar Heel State
I hope that extending a hand there
Will serve to heal a heart in Carolina
I hope that the floods of grief there
Will recede as he returns home
Rescuers and healers are needed
In every state

– August 2017

To a Young Man in a Coma

After Amy Gerstler

You haven't gulped down your allotted portion
of joy, so you must wake up. Recover,
and live for that something you yearn to do,
that somebody with whom you want to share
life lived fully, moments of true serenity
AND your allotted joy!
You've only used a small portion.
Find your way back to us.
Come from the basement you are in.
Climb those dark stairs and reenter
the squinty glare of consciousness. Grip
the rickety handrail.
Each of us has been there, held on before
with a hope that it and we will be strong enough.
Tell us your stories not yet told.
Ask for what is missing without
expectation it will immediately be yours.
You are not the first to trip and fall.
Come slowly up the stairs of life.
Reel in your soul, reel in reasonable hopes,
reel in your circles of care.
Receive and embrace their desire
That you live and love fully.
Surface, even if it feels like you're crashing
through plate glass doors. There's too much
left undone, unsaid, and in need of you
and your particular skills and gifts.
I need you to grow older with me
To grow older without me

– September 2017

Prompted by a poem by Amy Gerstler "To a Young Woman in a
Coma," From *Medicine* (2000, New York: Penguin Books). Gerstler's
poem prompted me to revisit my thoughts, feelings and wailing as
Chris lay gravely ill in the days preceding his untimely death.

What the Bee Sees

A photographer friend does the unusual
He takes photos of flowers from the perspective of a bee
He dives deep inside
Beyond the colorful bud
The surrounding leaves
To see the inner heart of a flower
What the bee sees

I wished for such a camera
I wished for abilities not possessed
I wished for clairvoyance
I wondered how my grandson saw himself
His inner and outer self

What would I have seen
Had my grandson let me inside
Beyond his hardening shell
Beyond his lovable, attractive surface
To his inner voice of yearnings
Wounds of shattered dreams
His desires about relationships

Where was his nectar and pollen
What fed his soul, spirit, body
I'm full of questions, sadness
For my grandson searches no longer
For nectar, pollen or people
I'm stung by his dying
Never seeing what he saw

I want to tell him what I saw
From all my vantage points
I want him to know the beauty
I came upon from his early flowering
Like a bee, I wanted to see inside his flower
Even though I deeply loved the outer layers

              – September 2017
with keen appreciation to Bernie Saunders, photographer.
Go to: *www.berniesaundersphotography.com*

Two Christophers

What if my two Christophers had met
I can only imagine now that both are dead
Two striking men separated by age
Countries, social circles, and life choices
Each left a lasting mark on me

I have often imagined friends I have
In the same setting for a few hours at least
Strangers upon arrival, I the only common thread
Oh to listen as they share their stories
What a gift it would be
Leaving they, nor I, would ever be the same

What if my two Christophers had met
One, an English gentleman in demeanor
But, so wonderfully accessible a force
Tall, handsome, full of curiosity
He welcomed me into his life
His family became family-like to me

The other, a young restless seeker
Athlete though modest about his skills
Unlike the other, this Christopher was a follower
Welcoming many into his life
As did the older Christopher
How I wish the elder's internal core
Could have rubbed off on my grandson
That they too had become family-like

I give thanks for each and both
I wanted both to live longer
I wanted each to die differently
Parkinson's took one; drugs the other
I was able to tell my English friend my love
Before he died
I conveyed my love to my grandson

Before he died
One I know heard it
That I said it is enough
Two Christophers; a poem of love

– October 2017

Getting Through...Life

Dearly beloved
We are gathered here today
To get through this thing called 'life'
from "Let's Go Crazy," by Prince

Oh, Prince, I want to sing along with you
I do for the first stanza
Life, life...gathered with others
I need all the help I can get
I love your use of the WE word

Life is crazy, yes
For you, for my grandson, it was
Each of you died of an overdose
Did you both go crazy?
I feel crazy more often than desired
This is not about judgement
This is about mysteries
About love, music, and crossroads
Where pain, suffering converge
I'm still on the road
Trying to get through life
Trying to see the sun, day or night
Awaiting what tomorrow brings
Confident, with beloveds, I will make it
I miss each of you

– October 2017

A Place with Distractions

Where to eat, a question with multiple answers
You choose, I said, choose comfort food this time

Turn here, he said, pointing toward Mac's Ribs
Upon entering, I thought it a strange choice
Noisy, busy, a sports bar with multiple screens

I followed the hostess to our table
We ordered our drinks, began perusing the menu
His beer, my wine arrived; we lifted our glasses
Saluted one another and acknowledged Ozzie
David's dog and companion

As we awaited our food, he explained his choice
Tonight, I needed a place with distractions

For over twelve hours, he had been preoccupied
Worried about the health of his long-time companion
Lethargy was the way it began
His lack of zeal for food, ready to do his "business"
Unresponsive to his master, with licks and attention
Were strange behaviors, Ozzie was not himself
The worries continued, calls to a vet followed

Ozzie was fourteen years old, three-legged
For half those years, but not handicapped
He was faithful, fun, and a constant friend
My son has had many loves; Ozzie was one of them

The care by the vet of Ozzie and my son was exemplary
He was gentle, honest, thorough and patient
Ozzie's organs were failing, the prognosis not good
This day contained a threshold we did not want to cross

This death was on-time, on-dog-time
The earlier one was off-time, complicated
Together, they pushed us all to the edge
Of living and dying, past and future stories

– December 2017

I Cry a Lot

I cry a lot these days.
It is said that older men cry more as they age
Older body parts or altered past patterns
Allow for release of tears

Grief, I have found, permeates, morphs, surprises
Some describe being ambushed by their grieving
Others know the triggers of obvious stimuli
That can be deliberate or surprise occurrences
The emotional movie, anniversaries
Whether predictable, chosen or ambushed
I cry a lot these days.

The obvious prompt is Chris' death
Now nine months past but ever present
A grandfather is not supposed to bury a grandchild
If the tears could speak, their messages would include
Deep loss, regret, missing him, and sadness
That I also cry when not remembering Chris
Tells me there is much for which to be sad these days
A man's hard drive can hold a lot of pain
I cry for the state of our world
The loss of civility, disregard for the marginalized
The deaths of friends, family members, strangers
My grief is highly personal and collective
As I wrestle with losses I invite
Chris the wrestler, to tell me his moves
I don't want to be taken down by loss
When I feel "gassed" or in the "bottom position"
Let me keep "grinding", find a "bridge"
Let me get back on my feet
Ready to cry some more.

– Late January/early February 2018

Permanent

...One word, hiding in my unconscious, lying in wait on the periphery of my knowledge... *Permanent*.
Claudia Osborn, brain-injured surgeon

For eleven months, I have been slowly absorbing that word,
The one on the periphery of my awareness
Permanent
To be sure, I knew my grandson would never be the same
As soon as I walked into the ICU and saw his body
Covered by and hooked to tubes, monitors, his life fading

The doctor's brain was severely injured
My heart was permanently broken
Knowing it there and then
Is not the same as I know it here and now
Permanent was immediate and now is chronic
Like the doctor I'm learning to live with something
I had hoped I would never face

Permanent, I am learning, does not mean dominant
Yes, triggers at strange and predictable times and places.
My life has been altered...permanently
Even so, broken hearts, while scarred,
Can still throb, keeping me alive
I had wished that my grandson made other choices
Now, I must practice what I preached to him
Choose despair or live as fully a life as I can
With ambiguity, ambivalence and loss
Chris had a broad smile that was contagious
His smile and mine, plus tears can live together
In perpetuity
                                        – March 2018

From *Over my head: A doctor's own story of head injury from the inside looking out*, by Charlotte Osborn

A Childless Granddad

It was the fourth repeat that got to me
My whole body leaned against the pew
Even as tears emerged from deep inside
Her voice, its cadence, strong while crying
Prompted something visceral, unexpected
The familiar yet startling words
"Sometimes I feel like a motherless child"
Not once, but steadily, slowly
That one line repeated pierced me

Earlier that week
The mother of Paris almost died
Notre Dame burned
Its potential absence found voice
"Sometimes I feel like a motherless child"

One year earlier my grandson died
His voice, his cadence, strong grandson
Hushed, but still repeatedly heard
Sometimes I feel like a childless dad
His potential gone, his fire quenched

Her voice strong, beautifully raw
Cried out my laments
Mothers, fathers, too many friends
And a beloved grandson
"Sometimes I feel like a motherless child"
Sometimes I know I am a childless granddad
Sing it again, four times

– April 2018

If in a Rush

If, in a rush,
And little could be taken,
I would want something sensual
Some things to touch, smell, see, hear
Brahms' Quartet in C
My grandson's painting, just received,
A small box from my wife's collection
The smell of coffee beans
Flannel sheets
My special footrest
A good poetry book
The sweater my dad wore
A cardinal from mom's stash

If, not rushed,
If slowly moving through the day
The list would remain
Though now expandable
Apples, hugs, hymns,
A lover's odor

Getting Along

Every person is like a piece of paper and each passerby
leaves a mark

(Chinese proverb)

The teacher gently asserted:
I've met lots of adults in my life.
Most could read or write,
Some had math skills,
All were potty-trained and,
I have met too many adults,
Who did not know how to get along with others.
If you wish to enroll your child
In this pre-school
We will include attention to math,
The language arts, including reading,
AND we will emphasize getting along.
Would you like to enroll your child?

Later, at her memorial,
Pride and appreciation were voiced
For the marks she left on children and parents
Her example and emphases affirmed
A tall man read from a piece of paper.
To work in this way with children
He proclaimed
Was radical social justice.

I left with awe, regret and envy.
I can add, subtract, write and read

In remembrance of Sheila Richter

Internal Roadmaps

I traveled recently down a path
Familiar but not recognizable

Strange isn't it
How seasoned travelers
Professional journeymen
Can forget or lose their maps
I knew grief was up ahead
But when I got there, I did not recognize it.

Like an Uncle

Emerging from the ice cream store, an inviting bench in sight, I knew this was the time to try and clarify our relationship. We had been talking about our "new family" as we had approached the store; the time seemed ripe. Grasping for words to express the confusing feelings and thoughts that had been bubbling inside me for weeks, I blurted out my question, "Beth, when you think about me or describe me to your friends, what words do you use? What do you say?"

Thoughtful my then 12 year-old stepdaughter paused and emotionally blurted out, "I'm glad you haven't tried to replace my father. I would have gotten mad about that."

"But if I'm not a father, what am I? Who am I to you?"

It was then that the ingenuity of children to make sense of confusion showed itself again. "Well, sometimes you're sort of like an uncle or an older brother, to which she added with a grin, a much older brother. And sometimes I think of you like an adult friend."

"Thank you," I said, "I'll take all of those as a compliment."

While the conversation continued, this part of it has lingered with me. It represents more than the growing, early relationship between two particular people, my stepdaughter and me. It is also the centuries old ritual of naming and fitting people together in relationships. While a similar ritual occurs in most relationships, it has become especially common and important in stepfamilies. Legally unattached except through the birthparent, stepchildren and stepparents frequently seek ways to make sense of their new connections. My sons asked me shortly after my marriage to the woman who then became their stepmother, "Dad, if you died, what would we be to Marge (my wife) and Beth and Brian (my stepchildren)?" They were trying to figure out—in developmentally concrete ways—their current and future ties to the people that had been added to their lives, now also called family.

Even though a special challenge in stepfamilies, the search and need for clarity about relationships is universal. My father wondered about his relationship with his wife of over 65 years as her memory loss deepened. Former peers wonder about their relationships after one gets a promotion and is now a supervisor. The disciples wondered about their relationship with Jesus. And Jesus, in turn, wondered what words they used to describe him. Many in Northern Ireland wonder about their current and future relationships with the onset of peace. "Who are we to each other now" seems to be a common question.

I have a T-shirt on which there is a picture of a panda in the pouch of a kangaroo and the words, "I Am A Stepparent." Years after my conversation with Beth, a colleague offered me and my children a wonderful image when he said that children in stepfamilies could be some of the luckiest of children by having more than two loving parental adults who love and care for them. I wish I could have said something like that while my new daughter and I ate ice cream long ago. I hope my stepfamily experiences will aid me in knowing that there are many ways of connecting. Lions and lambs can lie down together. Kangaroos can carry pandas. And stepparents can be unusual but loving uncles.

Holding the Chaos Gently

The dying man
Asked the psychiatrist to hold him
Gently, he did so
The embrace held man and memories
Too many people killed in the war
Too much life taken by a now dying veteran
His secrets held by another
Finally
Ready
The man died the next day

That's How It Began

I sometimes date it with the sit-in
Greensboro, a Woolworrth's, twenty-five miles from home
When black coffee was not served to black patrons
That image hard to swallow
Was that when my stirring began?

Could it have been as my father and I
Drove to pick up vegetables from farmers
Through one part of our town
To another part of our town
Separate, different, distinct
Intriguing, curious, and off-limits?

Could it have begun
When I first wondered about Uncle Willie
Loyal customer in the store
Familiar neighbor from down the road
Buying no more, no less than most
But, no one else was called Uncle?

When a pot is stirred, something happens
The boy's what was bumped into his what is
It finally dawned on him, this is so wrong
Stirred by King, Rosa, and Willie
The slow learner began to wake up

That's how it began
No burning bush
No quick conversion
Ever so slowly eyes widened
Heart opened, values clarified
What was should not be what is

That's how it began

Royalty

The man sitting alone in the restaurant
Had he asked for service for one
Attention to be paid only him

And, if so, had the wait staff cleared the restaurant
Quickly disbursed confused diners
Giving him the privacy he desired

Or had he come in at the wrong hour
One of those in-between-sittings times

Did the locals know something about this place
This stranger could not know until after eating

Whatever the reason
He sat like a king receiving the services
A man of his status deserved

Some years earlier, after a glorious concert in Amsterdam,
My wife and I stopped at a restaurant
Only to see the staff closing down for the evening
As we turned to leave, the owner escorted us back inside
The staff returned to their appointed stations
As we two received their elegant and unhurried care
The only customers to be seen

Everyone should be a king or queen at least for one meal
Everyone should sit tall like the solitary man
Like the couple enthralled earlier with music
Filled in due course with hospitality flavored food
Flushed with regal embarrassment

Glee to Start the Day

The glee of a ninety-one-year-old man who, five days late, has just had a bowel movement is unmatchable, its only comparison, the toddler, who has achieved similar success. Toothless, rubbing the sleep out of his eyes, but with a gleam on his face, my dad slowly moved around the corner of the kitchen and announced his overnight success. His grin and delight filled the kitchen and caressed his son who had worried most of the night how the next day would begin. Dad announced with gusto that he had almost awoken Mom and me at 3:00 am with the news of his release. And then, showing the depth of meaning this event had for this aging man, he reported that he had reached into the toilet just to touch what he had waited so long to see. He firmly hugged me, his smile wrapped around my body, and proclaimed that I could fix whatever I wanted for the family breakfast. He would not be in charge; I was the chief cook, for at least one day. And off he went to dress for his best day in a long time.

Caregiving children need such moments to remind them that basic bodily functions frequently dominate the daily lives of many elders. We, who know so little of marathon constipation, still have most of our own teeth, can rise out of chairs with relative ease, and who foresee a future of possibilities, can be out of touch with a harsh reality. I'm reminded of Cornelius Eady's haunting poem in which the dying father glares at the caregiving son *with the anger that the sick have for what a healthy body cannot know.* That morning in the kitchen was more than a humorous Kodak moment of delight, this was a teaching moment about aging. My dad knew something I did not yet know.

"Going Down Slow" from *You don't miss your water: Poems* (1995) by Cornelius Eady. New York: Henry Holt and Company, p. 23.

Father's' Day

I have no Father's Day Card to send this year!

Even though I stood and read the many choices
At many racks, in many stores, many times
I have not signed my name or written a message
This year.

My father died 36 days ago!

What does one do when habits or traditions
Lose their reason?
Does one send a card to all the fathers he sees
To the sons who have become fathers,
To the surrogates that have been father-like,
To the dead father who might still be listening,
To the muse that links fathers to sons to fathers and their sons,
Or to the mom that shared life with the man for 68 years?

One of my condolence cards called me an orphan
An odd label for one as old as me.
Others wrote of my longevity genes
A dad of 93 is not yet common
Whatever I am, I am lonely
I miss him and the ritual of cards
I don't like standing in stores unsure of the etiquette.
Pondering a ritual and habit now ending
With no champagne or graveyard nearby.

Oh Ted, Ted, Ted

Oh Ted, Ted, Ted,
Don't let the way others are treating me
Get in the way of what you and I can do while here

She was the famous therapist
Others seemed to be in awe of her
Their adulations dominated early training sessions

She sat at my lunch table
Just the two of us
Asked how the month-long workshop was going
I told her of my displeasure
The month of training had become days of fawning
I swallowed, already packing my departure bags
It was at that moment I experienced therapy at its best
It was all of forty-five seconds
Worth the cost of the whole month
Ted, Ted, Ted
Don't let the way others are treating me
Get in the way of what you and I can create

It was a life lesson, remembered now
Learned then, practiced often
But not often enough
Ted, Ted, Ted

Cultivating Gratitude

With appreciation to columnist Ellen Goodman

Years ago, the columnist wrote appreciatively of her man
The one doing so much more than earlier men would ever do
She was grateful

And she was mad
Expected womanly reminder traditions
Had collided with long-held male patterns
Pick up milk and get toilet paper seemed obvious
Grateful began to grate

Gratitude can expire like the slow leak of a tire
Relationships erode over time
Her words keep stirring
When patterns persist
It can be a foretelling of things to come
Unless and until I truly repair the leak

The male I was would think this poem strange
The man that male became is grateful it is

Acknowledgements

The following poems or prose pieces appeared earlier in these books or journals. The versions in this volume may be slightly modified.

"A Man's Tears" in *Journal of Poetry Therapy* (Winter 1990).

"Acorns, Bcorns and Ccorns" and "The Walk" in *A Walk with Nature: Poetic Encounters that Nourish the Soul* (2019) edited by Moats, M., Sebree, Jr., Belton, G., and Hoffman, L. Colorado Springs: *www.universityprofessorspress.com* Also in *Autumn* (2021) edited by Ruth Burgess, Glasgow: Wild Goose Publications.

"Changing Places" in *Lombardi Voices* (Fall 2005), then in *Bundles of Bog Cotton* (2015) edited by Butler, L Anderson. M. and Durkin, T. Glasgow: PlaySpace Publications.

"Chronic Smiling," "Father's Day," "Glee To Start the Day," "Like an Uncle," "Royalty," "Teeter-Totters and Caring," and "Unexpected Writer" in *Crossroads: Stories at the Intersections* (2008). Bethlehem, PA: Interprovincial Board of Communication, Moravian Church in America.

"Fatherhood" as an "Introduction" (2018) *The Road by Heart: Poems of Fatherhood*. Edited by Greg Watson and Richard Broderick. Minneapolis: Nodin Press and *Crossroads: Stories at the Intersections* (2008). Bethlehem, PA: Interprovincial Board of Communication, Moravian Church in America.

"If in a Rush" in *Bundles of Bog Cotton* (2015) edited by Butler, L Anderson. M. and Durkin, T., Glasgow: PlaySpace Publications.

"Internal Roadmaps" in *Journal of Pastoral Care* (1987).

"Like an Uncle" in *Nurturing News* (September 1985), then adapted in *Crossroads: Stories at the Intersections* (2008). Bethlehem, PA: Interprovincial Board of Communication, Moravian Church in America.

"Male Tears" in *The Journal of Pastoral Care* (Spring 1990).

"Pilgrimage Home" in *Fire and Bread* (2007) edited by Ruth Burgess, Glasgow: Wild Goose Publications.

"Safe Places" *in Voices: The Art and Science of Psychotherapy* (Fall 1991).

"Soften the Blow" in *The Wind Blows, The Ice Breaks* (2010) edited by Bowman, T. and Johnson, E., Minneapolis: Nodin Press and in *Crossroads: Stories at the Intersections* (2008). Bethlehem, PA: Interprovincial Board of Communication, Moravian Church in America.

"The Call" and "Two Weeks Ago" in *Coalition News*, June 2017.

"The Message" in *Bundles of Bog Cotton* (2015) edited by Butler, L Anderson. M. and Durkin, T., Glasgow: PlaySpace Publications and in *It Starts With Hope* (2016) edited by Brown, B. and Bowman, T., Minneapolis: Nodin Press.

"What the Bee Sees" and "Letting Go" in *Coalition News*, March 2018.

About the Author

Ted Bowman is a father, stepfather and grandfather. His family roots are in North Carolina. He has lived in Minnesota since 1973.

His work as a family and grief educator has occurred in Minnesota, many states, nine countries, including over twenty years of annual work in England, Scotland and Ireland beginning in 1996.

He is the author of more than 125 articles, chapters, booklets, and poems. His two booklets, *Loss of Dreams: A Special Kind of Grief*, published in 1994, and *Finding Hope When Dreams Have Shattered*, published in 2001, are widely used for grief and loss. *Crossroads: Stories at the Intersections*, a book of poems and essays was published in 2008. A co-edited (Elizabeth Bourque Johnson) volume of poetry, all by Minnesota poets addressing themes of loss and renewal, *The Wind Blows, The Ice Breaks*, was released in 2010. Ted was also co-editor of *It Starts with Hope* (with Betsy Brown) a volume of images and words for the 30th anniversary of The Center for Victims of Torture (CVT) in 2016.

His website is *www.bowmanted.com*.
His email is *tedbowman71@gmail.com*.

Made in the USA
Monee, IL
17 January 2024

51267731R00049